This Louisiana Thing That Drives Me

The Legacy of Ernest J. Gaines

This Louisiana Thing That Drives Me

The Legacy of Ernest J. Gaines

Reggie Scott Young, Marcia Gaudet, Wiley Cash
with introduction by Ernest J. Gaines

University of Louisiana at Lafayette Press

2009

University of Louisiana at Lafayette Press

© 2009 by University of Louisiana at Lafayette Press
P.O. Box 40831
Lafayette, LA 70504-0831

ISBN-10: 1-887366-83-0
ISBN-13: 978-1-887366-83-0

Library of Congress Cataloging-in-Publication Data

This Louisiana thing that drives me : the legacy of Ernest J. Gaines / Reggie Scott Young ... [et al.] ; with introduction by Ernest J. Gaines and an original poem by Wendell Berry.
p. cm.
ISBN-13: 978-1-887366-83-0 (alk. paper)
ISBN-10: 1-887366-83-0 (alk. paper)
1. Gaines, Ernest J., 1933---Homes and haunts--Louisiana. 2. Novelists, American--20th century--Biography. 3. African American authors--Biography. 4. Louisiana--In literature. 5. Louisiana--Biography. I. Young, Reggie Scott.

PS3557.A355Z48 2009
813'.54--dc22

2008023738

Printed on acid-free paper in China by Everbest Printing Company through Four Colour Imports, Ltd., Louisville, Kentucky.

This book is dedicated to all who lived in Cherie Quarters.

Ernest J. Gaines

Contents

from "Miss Jane and I," (*Callaloo*, 1978), by Ernest J. Gaines

I wanted to smell that Louisiana earth, feel that Louisiana sun, sit under the shade of one of those Louisiana oaks, search for pecans in that Louisiana grass in one of those Louisiana yards next to one of those Louisiana bayous, not far from a Louisiana river. I wanted to see on paper those Louisiana black children walking to school on cold days while yellow Louisiana busses passed them by. I wanted to see on paper those black parents going to work before the sun came up and coming back home to look after their children after the sun went down. I wanted to see on paper the true reason why those black fathers left home — not because they were trifling or shiftless — but because they were tired of putting up with certain conditions. I wanted to see on paper the small country churches (schools during the week), and I wanted to hear those simple religious songs, those simple prayers — that true devotion. . . . And I wanted to hear that Louisiana dialect — that combination of English, Creole, Cajun, Black. For me there's no more beautiful sound anywhere — unless, of course, you take exceptional pride in "proper" French or "proper" English. I wanted to read about the true relationship between whites and blacks — about the people that I had known.

Ernest J. Gaines

A Letter

(to Ernest J. Gaines)

Dear Ernie,

I've known you since we were scarcely
more than boys, sitting as guests
at Wallace Stegner's table, and I have read
everything you have written since then
because I think what you have written
is beautiful and quietly, steadily
brave, in the manner of the best bravery.
I feel in a way closer to your work
than to that of anybody else of our age.
And why is that? I think it's because
we both knew the talk of old people,
old country people, in summer evenings.
Having worked hard all their lives long
and all the long day, they came out
on the gallery down in your country,
out on the porch or doorstep in mine,
where they would sit at ease in the cool
of evening, and they would talk quietly
of what they had known, of what
they knew. In their rest and quiet talk
there was peace that was almost heavenly,
peace never to be forgotten, never
again quite to be imagined, the peace
above all else that we have longed for.

Wendell Berry

The photographs I've taken remind me of a time, remind me of a place, and of a people, that I write about. Without those photographs, I don't know that I could recall as accurately the things that I'd like to write about.

INTRODUCTION
BY ERNEST J. GAINES

In the early 1960s many of my friends were leaving San Francisco to write their novels. They could no longer live and write in this highly commercial world. They went to Europe, to Africa, to Mexico—some even went to Asia. My friend Jim and his wife Carol went to Guadalajara, Mexico, the summer of 1962, and I was supposed to go with them. But I told tell them that I'd have to hold on to my job a little longer because I needed more money and that I would join them in the fall or winter. I was having as much trouble writing my first novel as anyone.

But something happened in the fall of '62 which prevented me from going to Mexico and would change my life forever. James Meredith, the first black to enroll at the University of Mississippi, made international news. It was on television, on radio, in the newspapers every day. Most times it was the leading story on the six o'clock news with Chet Huntley and David Brinkley on one channel, and Walter Cronkite on the other. And each night one or the other looked directly at me when they spoke of the harassments and threats to death this young man suffered every hour he was at that university. Especially Walter Cronkite. He would find me in the room surrounded by family or friends and speak directly to me. Soon my family and friends were doing the same thing. They knew that I was trying to write a novel of the South. They knew as I knew why I didn't want to go back there. Because of the civil rights demonstrations, there was much violence throughout the South.

They did not blame me for not wanting to go back. But if I didn't want to go back, why frustrate myself trying to write a novel about the South. Why not write about something else? I had tried to write about other subjects—an interracial love story, a ghost story, a story about bohemian life in San Francisco, a story about my army experience—but none of them rang true. The heart was there, but not the soul. So I wrote to Jim and Carol informing them that I would not join them in Mexico, but I had to go back home to write my novel. I telephoned my uncle and aunt in Baton Rouge, and asked them if I could visit them for a while. On January 3, 1963, a friend drove me to the train station in Oakland, California, and 48 or 50 hours later my uncle met me at the train station in Baton Rouge. I've told people in the past that two of the greatest moves I've ever made in my life were when I left Louisiana in 1948, and when I returned to Louisiana in 1963. Because I could not attend high school or enter a library in my part of Louisiana, my parents took me to California to be educated. Because James Meredith entered the University of Mississippi 15 years later, I decided to come back. I had returned to Louisiana twice before but for only a week or two. This time I decided to stay for six months or a year.

Every Sunday my uncle and aunt and two others who lived in the house and I would drive out to the country, the old place, the plantation, where we had all come from. We would visit relatives who had prepared lunch of chicken, or stewed beef, with rice and greens. It could be mustard or collard or cabbage, and there would be cornbread, and cake for dessert. And we would sit and ask God to bless the food, and after we had eaten I would go back in the fields, and I would find a stalk of sugarcane and peel it with my knife, and chew it, and let some of the sweet juice run down my chin as I had done as a child. I would search for pecans under one of the many pecan trees, and crack the pecan shell with my teeth as I had done

fifteen, sixteen, twenty years ago. Then I would go into the cemetery where my ancestors were buried, and listening to the wind rustling the pecan and oak tree leaves, I would feel better at that moment than I ever felt in San Francisco. Looking around at the different graves and at the trees and the cane fields beyond the cemetery, I realized now why I could not write my novel in San Francisco. I could not get the true feeling of the place until I came back.

By nine o'clock each weekday everyone else had left the house, and I had the rest of the day to think and write. And my characters were beginning to do what they were supposed to do and talked the way they were supposed to talk and interact with each other as they were supposed to. And the flowers began to bloom at the right time, and trees began to have leaves at the right time of spring, and the rain fell at a certain time and stopped at a certain time in the evening—and I knew all of this was happening because James Meredith had made me come back to Louisiana.

Six months later I returned to San Francisco to finish writing my novel. I wanted to put everything in the novel that I had learned the past six months and all I could remember of what the people had talked about. But when I sent the novel to New York, my editor told me to take most of it out and stick to the simple love story about the Creole girl and her dark skinned lover. He told me the other stuff was good, but it should be put into another book.

I grew up on a plantation in Pointe Coupée Parish in South Louisiana. Until I was fifteen years old, I was raised by a lady who never walked in her life—my aunt, Miss Augusteen Jefferson. She crawled over the floor and the yard for fifty some years. Still she could look after my other brothers and me. She cooked our food. We had to bring everything to her while she sat on a bench by the wood-burning stove. She had another little bench in front of her where she cut up the vegetables or the meat before putting the food into one of the pots on the stove. She washed our clothes. We brought the washtub, the washboard, the soap and water to her, while she sat on her little bench and braced herself on the rim of the tub and rubbed the clothes on the washboard. When she had finished washing and rinsing the clothes, we hung the clothes on a wire line out in the yard. My aunt also patched our clothes when they were torn or worn out. She also disciplined us when we did something wrong. We had to break our own switch and get down on our knees before her to take our punishment. After she had taken her afternoon nap, she would crawl over the porch, down the steps, into her vegetable garden. Other times she would crawl over the back yard to search for pecans under the tree.

Because my aunt couldn't visit other people on the plantation, the people would always come to our house. There they would talk, and talk, and talk and talk. While three or four of them sat on the floor sewing on a quilt, they would talk. While they sat on the floor picking twigs out of moss to stuff mattresses, they would talk. While they shelled beans or peas or cut okra or peeled pecans, they would talk. Sometimes they would just talk and talk while they drank strong sweet black coffee. And because none of them had gone to school, I had to write their letters to relatives and friends. They knew the first line or two of the letter, but I had to create the rest. I talked about the garden, I talked about the field, I talked about the church—who had had a baby, who had found religion, who had been baptized, who had died, who was in the hospital or in jail. If they liked what I had written, I was paid with a nickel or with tea cakes and clabber. If they didn't like what I had written, I had to erase it and start all over again. I did this until I went to California in 1948. Twenty years later, in 1968, I got the idea to write a novel about what I thought they had talked about those many days out on the porch and those many nights inside by the fireplace.

After my stay in Baton Rouge in 1963, I would return to Louisiana twice a year—late winter or spring for the Mardi Gras, and again in the fall for the Bayou Classic between the Southern University and Grambling University football teams. I would always visit the old place, the plantation where I had lived as a child. My aunt was dead now, and many of the old people for whom I had written letters were dead now, but there were still some around. I would come back to the old place and talk to them. Mr. Reese Spooner and Mr. Walter Zeno were two of them. Mr. Zeno liked his wine, so I would get a half-gallon of wine to take to him. Reese didn't drink. I would stand out on the porch listening to them talk about the old days. They knew everything that had happened since the turn-of-the-century. They knew my grandparents' grandparents. They knew the horses they rode, they knew the clothes they wore, they knew when they had died, and where they were buried.

I reminded them of the *collage à trois* of Booker T. Washington, Frederick Douglass, and Abraham Lincoln which hung against the wall in my aunt's room. Oh, they remembered that, that picture hung in many bedrooms to remind black people who had fought for them.

This led to the subject of when the Yankees left the South—according to their parents or grandparents—and how poor black people had to put up with the Klans and the night riders. I kept asking questions and more questions and we came into the 20th century. They talked about the great flood of '27. I asked about the great flood of '12. "Well, we just little bitty children then," but that one of '27, they would remember forever. Then tell me about it, I said.

They did not talk about year or month. They could not recall where the levee had breached. They talked about seasons, whether it was cold or warm, or whether the crop of cane or corn or cotton was good or bad that year. Of the great flood of '27, they did not know the year, but they did know that it was just before Huey P. Long came into power. And they can tell you the color of the water, and the animals and the trash that flowed on the surface of the water, and how quiet the water was, and how many days it lasted before they could return to their gardens or to the fields. To get the facts of date and breach of the levee, I had to visit Miss Evangeline

Lynch at the Louisiana Room at the LSU Library.

They talked about the life and death of Huey P. Long. Their Huey P. Long and the rich people's Huey P. Long and history's Huey P. Long were not the same person. To them, Huey P. Long was a friend of the poor. He was the first to give school books to black people. The books were hand-me-downs that white students had soiled, had torn out pages, had stuck pages together with chewing gum, but many of the pages were readable, and that was better than before when they had nothing.

They talked about Huey P. Long's death, and they did not believe that Dr. Weiss had killed him, but it was the rich people who had killed him because of what he did for the poor. They used to say, "Now why would Dr. Weiss kill him because somebody said that Dr. Weiss's wife had some black blood in the family? Everybody had some black blood in the family somewhere, and some white blood in the family if you was a black. No, Dr. Weiss didn't kill him—the rich people had paid guards to kill him. To prove it, now, the doctor didn't know how to operate on him right—to go in the front to dig out the bullets, or to go out in the back to dig out the bullets—they didn't want to dig out the bullets, they wanted him to bleed there and die—them rich white folks wanted that."

They could talk about the fight between Joe Louis and Max Schmeling—how mournful it was for them after the first fight, when Joe Louis had lost. How happy all of them were after Joe Louis knocked Max Schmeling out in the first round of the second fight. They all gathered around a single radio in the quarter to listen to the fight. And they could demonstrate how Joe

Louis had knocked Max Schmeling down, and how his legs had quivered while lying on his back. Whether the announcer on the radio had described the fight in this way or whether they had imagined it to have happened this way, I had no idea. I would have to go to the archives at LSU to get the facts.

Now we came up to the late thirties when I was six years old, and though I still listened to what they had to say, now I could remember things for myself. One of the first things I could remember was roasting sweet potatoes overnight in the hot ashes of the fireplace. These potatoes with a glass of milk would be my breakfast the next morning before going to school. Since I was the eldest of my siblings, and it was winter, it was my duty to get up first and light a fire in the fireplace so the floor would be warm when Auntie got up to start her work for the day.

After that, I went to school. School was the church where the people on the plantation worshipped on Sundays. Five to five-and-a-half months, between late October and early April, this was school. This was school when there was no work for small children to do in the field.

In school, we sat on benches where the older folks had sat on Sundays. There were no desks, so we lay our books in our laps. To write out our assignments, we either lay the piece of paper on top of our book, or we got down on our knees and used the seat of the bench as the desktop. Ventilation in the room was by way of the four windows on either side the church and from front and back doors. Our heat came from a wood-burning stove in the center of the church. The children of the lower grades sat nearest the heater, the larger children sat farther back. A dozen or fifteen families on the plantation sent their children to the school. One of the families would bring a load of wood at the beginning of the year and another family would bring another load of wood when it was necessary. The larger boys chopped the wood with axes, and the smaller children brought the wood into the school and stacked it against the heater. During my time there between primer and sixth grade, I did both. And just before Christmas the larger boys would go back into the field to find a bush big

enough for a Christmas tree. The girls would decorate the tree using tinsels for icicles, different colors of crepe paper for lights, and lint cotton for snow. The Christmas show was always a special event for the children and for their parents each year.

As we got older, eight and nine years old, we went out into the fields to pick up Irish potatoes, to pull onions in the spring, and to pick cotton in the late summer and fall. When cotton picking was over, we went back to school.

Since most people on the plantation had a vegetable garden beside or behind the house and raised their own chickens and their hogs, there was always a *boucherie* (hog butchering) at someone's house in the fall. Most of the young men had to participate at sometime in the *boucherie*—it was a kind of initiation into manhood. I hated it. The men would grab a hog, slam it down on the wooden pallet, and cut its throat. But it took two or three people to do this, and this is when I would be chosen. You had to hold the front legs or the hind legs, and I always tried to get the hind legs, as far away from the squealing as I could get. The blood from cutting the hog's throat was caught in an aluminum pan and taken into the house for blood pudding. Boiling water was poured on the carcass of the hog, and the hog was scraped clean with knives, and the meat was cut—some for crackling, some to be given away to the people on the plantation, and the rest to be salted down and kept for the winter. All the children on the plantation would gather to get a few pieces of crackling. For children, this was the best of the *boucherie*.

When I was eleven years old, two of my uncles, George and Horace, took me into the swamps to cut wood. My uncles would throw the tree, which meant cut it down to the ground, and then my Uncle George and I would saw, while my Uncle Horace would split the logs. It was a task I wouldn't wish on anyone, even my worst enemy. We went into the swamps in the early morning, six or seven o'clock, in July and August, the hottest time of the year. You fought mosquitoes from the time you got there, and you had to kill a snake every so often. You worked until about noon, then loaded the wagon with split wood and came back to the quarter. Later in the afternoon, I would go fishing with some of the other boys. If we didn't fish, we shot marbles or played ball.

Our favorite marble game was called knucks. Short for knuckles. Three holes about the size of a small teacup were dug into the ground in a straight-line, about six feet apart. A line about six or seven feet from the first hole was drawn, and each player lagged for the line. The one nearest was first to shoot, then on and on down the line. Then we shot our marbles to make the holes. The last player to make the hole had to put his fist down on the ground, and we had to throw at his fist. There could be three or four of us, there could be six or seven of us. The loser had to keep his fist to the ground until we threw at it. Sometimes he wouldn't, and that would cause a fight. Other times he took his punishment like a man, wishing he would get even next time. I am happy to say that I was pretty good at marble shooting, and my knucks very seldom came down. As a matter of fact, just before I left Louisiana in 1948, I buried a can of marbles in our back yard. In the late '80s or the '90s, when LSU was excavating the land, when they were removing the cabins from the quarters, someone found that can of marbles and told me about it, but I never got one of them.

Around our twelfth birthdays, the people on the plantation thought it was time for us to put aside our sinful ways and join the church. Stop playing ball, stop shooting marbles, and stop singing those sinful songs—and start praying for religion. Not all of us heeded that advice, but many of us did—boys and girls alike. We had to attend church every night. So we took baths in Number 3 washtubs in the backyard, put on our best clothes, and went up the quarters to the church. The church sat in the middle of the quarters, so you walked there in five or ten minutes easily. There the old people would pray for us sinners—how they would pray—the sisters of the church, the deacons, and the minister. The little sinners sat on the first bench, and the minister would come from the pulpit and put his hand on our heads while calling on God to help us throw over that burden of sin. We prayed along with him. When we were not at the church, but at home or out in the field, we still had to pray. We spent much time alone so we would not be distracted by that outside sinful world. We talked only when it was absolutely necessary; we hardly ever found anything funny to laugh about. Most of us found religion while picking cotton in the early afternoon around two o'clock, the hottest time of the day. Whenever you

found religion, or "came through," you were given the rest of the day off so you could go home and prepare your talk, your confession, to the church that night. Everyone who was able came to the church to hear the young convert's travels.

The travel usually found the young sinner on a dark, deserted road or in the swamps trying to find his way home. Not only was he or she lost, but they also carried heavy burdens on their backs. They kept falling, but getting up; falling and getting up. There were all kinds of traps in front of them—snakes crawling across the road, dogs growling and snapping at them. Men in masks held shotguns trying to keep them back, but they kept on praying and step-by-step moving forward until they saw the light, the brightest light that they'd ever seen. And there that heavy burden just slipped away from their backs, and they were safe at last. Some found religion in one week, in others it took two; and some did not get religion all that year, but promised to try again during the next revival.

After there were a substantial number of candidates, we in white robes went to the river to be baptized. We were taken to the water one at a time to about waist deep. There the minister prayed over each one

of us a moment, and then dipped us under. Returning to the bank, the congregation would sing and clap, thanking God for having saved another poor sinner. After we had gotten out of our wet clothes—the girls at one of the houses in the quarters, the boys at another—we were led back to church for holy communion. No wine, but a soft drink and a small piece of cracker. We were little Christians now. Some of us remained in the church, remained on that plantation. Many of us left—left for the town and the city. Some of them found success in the city, most did not. I was one of the lucky ones. My mother and stepfather who had gone to California during World War II, sent me a ticket to join them. I was fifteen.

I can still remember how the people gathered at my aunt's house the day I left for California, the old people for whom I had written letters sitting on the porch, and the boys and girls either sitting on the steps to the porch or playing out in the yard. But they were there to see me off.

I was inside the house packing the old brown leather suitcase that my Uncle George had given me. There wasn't much to pack, but it took hours to do so. I couldn't have had more than two pairs of extra pants except for the pair I was wearing. I couldn't have had more than two extra shirts, one for dress, the other for everyday wearing. I must have had another pair of shoes, a pair of long johns, and a pair of undershirts and shorts. Not much else. Maybe a light jacket or sweater. And that would have been the limit of my clothing. Then I had to pack the food that the old people had brought for me—fried chicken, sliced bread, baked sweet potatoes, tea cakes, and probably pralines. All of this wrapped in brown paper bags to not soil my clothes. I must have packed and unpacked and repacked my clothing and food a half-dozen times. I must have

looked around the room that many times. I must have sat on the bed and cried quietly to myself that many times, before I went out on the porch to tell Auntie I was leaving. She sat on the floor outside the door where she always sat. The old people sat in chairs or on the floor, the children sat on the steps. They all got quiet when I came outside. "I'm going, Auntie," I said. I didn't get down on the floor to hug her, or get down on the floor to kiss her, or reach for her hand. All I said was "I'm going, Auntie." But what I wanted to say was, "Don't let me go, Auntie. Don't let me leave you, don't let me leave my home." But I could see in her face, as sad as that face was, that I had to go. I would be the first male in the history of the family to go beyond elementary school. So I had to go. "I'll make you proud of me, Auntie," I said to myself. "I swear, I'll make you proud of me."

I went to the old people who sat on the porch to tell them I was leaving. They raised their hands to mine. Most of them nodded and were quiet. But one said to me, "Just remember where you come from."

The children on the steps and in the yard followed me to the highway where I used my handkerchief to flag down the Trailway bus. I climbed on and walked down the aisle till I passed the little sign that read "White" on one side and "Colored" on the other, and then I found a seat holding my suitcase in my lap. At the bus terminal in New Orleans, I was given instructions how to get to the train station which would take me to California. Two and a half days later I was in Crockett, California, and there I would get a taxi to take me across the bay to my new home, Vallejo.

Like any healthy 15 or 16-year-old boy, after school I liked hanging around with my friends until my stepfather, who was in the merchant marine, came home on one of his vacations and told me to stay off the block or I would get myself into trouble. I had three other choices—the movie theater, the YMCA, or the library. I had no money, so the movie theater was out. And I chose to go to the YMCA. One day one of the guys at the Y asked me if I'd like to box. I knew nothing about the art of boxing, but I had nothing else to do, so I got into the ring. My opponent used every trick of the trade of boxing and by halfway through the second round, he had hit me everywhere on my body that it was legal to hit a man. So I was the one who originated the rope-a-dope, not Muhammad Ali 30 years later. I used it in the second round of my first fight. I leaned back against the rope, and with my teeth I began to take off the gloves while all the guys stood around laughing. Too embarrassed to return to the YMCA, I found my way to the library. There I discovered books. Books and books and books everywhere. I began to read books. There were none in that library by black writers, so I would read the white writers. The American writers, the 19th-century Russian writers, the 19th-century French writers—if they wrote about the land, about peasant life, I would read them. I can even remember reading *The Good Earth* by Pearl Buck. I read it because "Earth" was part of the title. I would read anything that reminded me of the home I came from. But in none of the books did I find me, and it was then that I tried to write. I have been at the art of writing for over 50 years. Recently, while visiting a high school, a student asked me what point of view did I find easiest to write my novels. Without hesitating, I said the first-person point of view, and I realize now why I said that—I'm still writing those letters for the old people on that plantation. I've published eight books and all of the stories take place in that general area, but I still have not told all their stories. An elementary school student once asked me if I would write all my life. I told her that on my deathbed that I would have a pen and a clipboard in my lap. She said nobody dies like that anymore. Someone else asked me, since I spent most of my life in California, when I would write a novel about San Francisco. I said when all the Louisiana stuff is out of me—and I hope it never happens.

I want to write
about my people.
I heppud to come
from Louisiana and
I heppud to come
from the land.

LAND

Legend holds that the final year of the seventeenth century found Sieur d'Iberville exploring the woods of the lower Mississippi River with the plan of establishing a French colony for King Louis XIV. Legend also holds that he, while being led by Native American guides, followed the river until it almost doubled back upon itself, leaving behind a 22-mile-long oxbow lake and a secret passage through the woods that offered a shortcut between points along the river. In 1729, this area became the French Military post of Pointe Coupée, and the long, narrow lake that was easily mistaken for a river with no origin became known as *Fausse Riviere*, or the False River.

In the centuries that followed, Pointe Coupée would be governed under the flags of Bourbon France, Spain, Britain, the Republic of West Florida, the United States, the independent Republic of Louisiana, and the Confederate States of America. The population was a mixture of the Native Americans who originally inhabited the fertile land, the French and the Spanish who would arrive and conquer it, and the Africans who eventually would be forced to work it as slaves and later as sharecroppers. The land yielded sugarcane, cotton, corn, and rice, and the long growing season and the free labor of slaves encouraged the settlement of the land and the building of plantations that centralized the work force and offered easy living to the families of rich, white landowners.

Many of these sprawling plantations and beautiful antebellum homes still dot the countryside around False River, and on maps and in guide books you can find them under names like Parlange, Riverlake, and Alma. Scattered around the river you will find small towns like Livonia, Lakeland, Oscar, and New Roads. But what you won't find on any map is the small town of Bayonne, nor will you find listed on any census the people who populate it. This is because Bayonne is a place that exists only in the fiction of Ernest J. Gaines and in the imaginations of the people who have read his novels and stories. Yet, like William Faulkner's Yoknapatawpha County and Thomas Wolfe's Altamont, the Bayonne of Ernest J. Gaines is real, and if you walk north along the banks of the False River toward New Roads, you will find it.

What you won't find are the old cabins that once dotted the road that leads from Riverlake Plantation to Cherie Quarters where Gaines was born in 1933; nor will you find weary bodies bent to their work in the sugar cane fields. Instead you'll find men on large tractors and machines that do the cutting, pulling, and baling that just a few decades ago was done by human hands. You'll also find that the once empty river banks have given way to large, beautiful homes and weekend fishing camps that belong to folks from cities like Baton Rouge and Lafayette.

But, if you've read the work of Ernest J. Gaines, the place you'll find will be familiar because you've visited it before. During these visits, you've heard the sound of singing voices lifting from the tiny church that once sat in the middle of the quarters, the same church that rests now, restored and elegant, in Gaines' backyard. On your hands and knees, you've combed the high grass for fallen pecans that hide themselves amongst the marked and unmarked graves of slaves and sharecroppers in the cemetery nestled a quarter mile behind the still-standing master's house. You've watched children stamp up dust in the scorching summer sun, and you've seen them hide from the heat under sagging porches where they shoot marbles and bury their loot in the cool, shaded earth beneath the cabins. You know this place and you've seen these things because you've read the stories of Ernest J. Gaines. You know that it is a place where young men pull corn in dancing shoes, where centuries-old women talk to oak trees, and where even a tough-hearted schoolteacher can stand to learn one last lesson or two.

What you may not know is that a fifteen-year-old boy named E.J. once stood by the roadside waiting for the bus with one eye looking back down the quarters he had just left, and the other fixed wearily upon the road that stretched to California, and beyond to places he couldn't imagine. And what he didn't know then is that, years later, he would one day write stories that recreate the place that he had to leave and recapture a way of life that is now gone but, because of his stories, will always be.

R. Wiley Cash

I could use the plantation as home for my characters. I knew life on the plantation because I had written about it in several other books—*The Autobiography of Miss Jane Pittman*, *Of Love and Dust*, and the stories in *Bloodline*. I could use the church school for background, the church where generations of my folks had worshipped and where I had attended school my first six years. I could use the crop as background— when it was planted, when it was harvested. I knew the food the people ate, knew the kind of clothes they wore, knew the kind of songs they sang in the fields and in the church.

I had no choice as to where I would be born, but since I was born in the South, Louisiana is the greatest place I think any artist could be born because of its romantic history. I think coming from the South, I have experiences that maybe blacks or whites of any other race or nationality would not have if you were born and raised up in the Midwest. I think I'm closer to the earth, I'm closer to nature, and I'm closer to the different attitudes, both good and bad.

I made my home in glory;
I shall not be moved.

Made my home in glory;
I shall not be moved.

Just like a tree that's
planted 'side the water.

Oh, I shall not be moved.

"Just Like a Tree," *Bloodline.*

As a boy, I had "snatches" of happiness. I could do things on the plantation that needed to be done and that pleased me. But when I was around little girls, I was bashful. I never knew what to say to them and envied boys who did.

I did it for them under them trees. I did it 'cause that tractor is getting closer and closer to that graveyard, and I was scared if I didn't do it, one day that tractor was going to come in there and plow up them graves, getting rid of all proof that we ever was.

~ Johnny Paul, *A Gathering of Old Men*.

A recurring theme I deal with in so much of my fiction . . . is that blacks were taken out of Africa and separated traditionally and then physically here in this country. We know that on the slave block in New Orleans, or Washington, D.C., or Baltimore, or wherever the slave ships docked, families were separated. Mothers were separated from their children, husbands from their wives, fathers from their sons, mothers from their daughters. And I feel that because of that separation they still have not, philosophically speaking, reached each other again.

I think there is something about the river that connects Southern writing, just like there's something about the land. I grew up on False River . . . and we got about as much food from the river as we got from the earth.

There was a church not very far from our house. I could hear the people singing all the time. I had to go to Sunday school and church as a child, and, of course, the people sang. I could never carry a tune myself, but the old ones did.

While writing fiction, there are certain things that you can capture both in terms of language and situations that historical texts could never really render in terms of what actually happened. That's where the imagination plays a role.

Where the boy stands, he can see the road from which he has just left—the quarter. . . . An hour ago he was packing to leave. . . . After he had finished, he tied up his suitcase and looked around the room. His ancestors, who had once been slaves, lived, if not in this house, then in one just like this one in the quarter.

There's an old oak tree up the quarters where Aunt Lou Bolin and them used to stay. That tree has been here, I'm sure, since this place been here, and it has seen much much, and it knows much much. And I'm not ashamed to say I have talked to it, and I'm not crazy either.

~ Miss Jane, *The Autobiography of Miss Jane Pittman*.

My ties are here because of my writing. I was taken away when I was fifteen years old. I had to be taken away because I could not go to high school here. I couldn't go to the library, and my folks wanted me to be educated. I didn't want to leave, and I didn't want to leave my aunt who raised me. Something of me just stayed here. I was always coming back to Louisiana.

I don't know that the Christian religion will bring fathers and sons together again. I don't know that the father will ever be in a position . . . from which he can reach out and bring his son back to him again.

I came from a place where people sat around and chewed sugarcane and roasted sweet potatoes and peanuts in the ashes and sat on ditch banks and told tales and sat on porches and went into the swamps and went into the fields—that's what I came from.

I try to create stories out of something that could have happened, Or may have happened, or what men dream about doing.

LITERATURE

Porch Talk with Ernest Gaines

Conversations on the ... Writer's ...

Callaloo

Catherine Carmier

A NOVEL

Ernest J. Gaines

CRITICAL REFLECTIONS ON THE FICTION ...

ERNEST ...

BLOODLINE
ERNEST J. GAINES

A Lesson Before Dying

Ernest J. Gaines
Author of The Autobiography of Miss Jane Pitman

In My Father's House

ERNEST J.
A GATHERING OF
A NOVEL

of love and dust

ERNEST J. GAINES

...GRAPHY OF
...ane
...man

A NOVEL BY
Ernest J. G...

ERNEST J.
GAINES
Author of A LESSON BEFORE DYING

MOZART AND LEADBELLY
STORIES AND ESSAYS

During a recent visit to *La maison entre les champs et la rivière*, Ernest J. Gaines' residence on False River in Oscar, LA, Ernie surprised Marcia Gaudet and me by pulling out a new story, "My Uncle and the Fat Lady," and asked if we had time to hear him read it. No matter what we might have had on our agendas back at the university in Lafayette, we told him we had all the time in the world. We had no idea Ernie was busy at work writing, especially after his long hiatus from his work on the yet-to-be-completed *The Man Who Whipped Children*. After retiring from teaching and building a new house and settling it, finding the time to write seemed to be a more difficult task for Ernie than it had been in the past.

All of his previous novels and published stories had been written in San Francisco, even though they were all motivated by what he has described as "this Louisiana thing that drives me." However, he was not in San Francisco anymore and was now living in the midst of the land and culture that he made famous to the rest of the world through his writing. Other things had happened in recent years that also had to affect his comfort level as a writer: he lost his long time editor, Dorothea Oppenheimer, after the publication of *A Gathering of Old Men*, and she was not only the person who placed and promoted his work but someone who served as his ideal reader; he also married for the first (and last) time to Dianne Saulney Gaines, a New Orleans native who was an attorney in Miami at the time they met. Their marriage took place during the last stages of his work on *A Lesson Before Dying*. Due to the widespread acclaim of that novel, Ernest J. Gaines, labeled "A New Star in the Canon" by the *Chronicle of Higher Education*, found himself in such demand by colleges and universities, civic groups, Oprah, HBO Productions, his students, his family, and even by entire municipalities in One City/One Book programs in Seattle, Miami, Rochester, Cincinnati, Lafayette, and many others, that it would take years before he would be able to find a few free moments where he might once again be able to write.

There were also other changes that were taking place in his life that would prevent him from having the kind of solitude he had benefited from before he became labeled a certified star literary figure. Once he became a married and settled man, he had to have a dog and found himself with a rather demanding, although adorable one, DeeDee, and then a grandchild,

Annalisa. On top of that, there were negotiations with architects, contractors, and builders because retirement required a house, not only for him but also for the wife, grandchild, dog, and frequent visitors. Then, not long after the house was designed, built, and settled, along came Katrina which caused no damage to the house, but the house, being a big house with open doors, became a refuge and shelter for relatives and friends from all over south Louisiana who found themselves displaced by the storm. But then after the storm and after relatives and friends made their ways back to their own rebuilt homes or resettled in places of their own, when there was once again only Ernie and Dianne, and grandchild (mostly on weekends), and DeeDee the dog, it seemed—at least to us—as if the writing just would not come.

Just two years earlier, Marcia and I, possibly fearing something we would never express out loud—that Ernest J. Gaines might have written his last work of fiction—came up with the idea of *Mozart and Leadbelly*, Ernie's last published book. We knew readers wanted more from Gaines, but that there were also words he had written most people had not had an opportunity to read. To us, even if there were to be no new stories, long or short, we were happy because if you add up *Catherine Carmier*, *Of Love and Dust*, the *Bloodline* stories, *The Autobiography of Miss Jane Pittman*, *In My Father's House*, *A Gathering of Old Men*, *A Lesson Before Dying*, and the stories and published talks ("essays") that make up *Mozart and Leadbelly*—they equal more than anyone could want from a writer in a lifetime. He had already done his work, so it was now up to us to help preserve his legacy. That is one of the purposes of this book, and the reason why we are working to establish a center for the study of Ernest J. Gaines at the University of Louisiana at Lafayette. That's why Marcia and I went out to visit him the other day, to go over the proofs of the introductory essay he wrote for this volume and to consult with him concerning other aspects of this book. And then he broke out his new story, "My Uncle and the Fat Lady," and we sat there and listened with our mouths agape. We were a private audience hearing the first piece of new writing by Ernest J. Gaines in several years. We were both honored and flattered. Now we have to wonder if the purpose of this book will be to mark the next stage in his long and distinguished career as a writer.

Reggie Scott Young

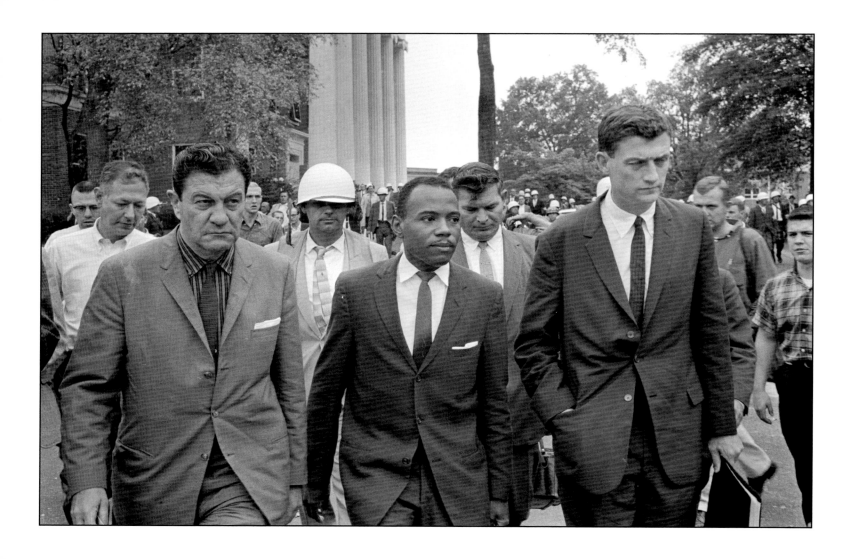

Something happened that summer of 1962 that would change my life forever. James Meredith enrolled at the University of Mississippi. Every night we watched the news . . . and it seemed that we cared for nothing else but the bravery of this one young man.

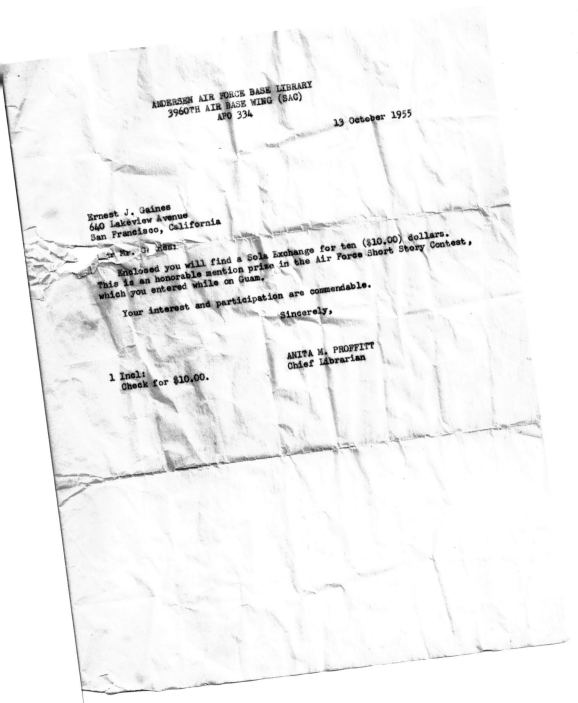

ANDERSEN AIR FORCE BASE LIBRARY
3960TH AIR BASE WING (SAC)
APO 334
13 October 1955

Ernest J. Gaines
640 Lakeview Avenue
San Francisco, California

Dear Mr. Gaines:

Enclosed you will find a Sola Exchange for ten ($10.00) dollars. This is an honorable mention prize in the Air Force Short Story Contest, which you entered while on Guam.

Your interest and participation are commendable.

Sincerely,

ANITA M. PROFFITT
Chief Librarian

1 Incl:
Check for $10.00.

While in the army, I tried to write in my off-duty hours, but I found that I liked shooting pool, and playing pinochle too much. All I got accomplished was a short story that was good enough to take second place on the island of Guam. The story was sent to our command headquarters in Japan to compete with all the other short stories by GIs in the Far East. There it got honorable mention.

47

THE TURTLES

When we got to Mr. James's house, my old mar
poles against the fence and we went into the y
Benny were sitting on the porch. Mr. James v
with his straw hat.

"It's coming down," my old man said. He pu
and leaned upon one knee. "You and Benny ab

"Aren't you and Max going to rest awhile?"

"Better not stop too long," my old man sa
starting again.'"

"I see what you mean," Mr. James said. "

"You want me to wake up Ma and te
asked.

"She knows we're going," Mr. James said

Benny went inside and got his hat, the
from beside the house. He got the can of w
where he kept them cool and moist, and v
Lake. Gillman's Lake was about two mil
and we made it over there way inside of

It was quiet and cool around the lake

77

Catherine Carmier

"A first-rate achievement in every sense."—San Francisco Chronicle

by the author of
A Lesson
Before Dying

ERNEST J. GAINES

After leaving the Army, I enrolled at San Francisco State to study English literature and creative writing. . . . I wrote a story I called "The Turtles," and later it would be the first story published in the San Francisco State literary magazine. Miss Dorothea Oppenheimer, who was just starting her literary agency in San Francisco, saw the story and liked it, and she was my agent until she died.

Writing for me is discovery. If I knew everything when I began to write a novel, I'm afraid it would be boring to write. I do not know everything that's going to happen. . . . I don't want to know everything. I want to discover, as you, the reader, want to discover, what it's all about.

Meet

ERNEST J. GAINES, *author*

*on Thursday Evening
at the Western Addition
Branch Library
Geary and Scott
November 2nd at 8 p.m.*

Mr. Gaines' new novel OF LOVE AND DUST will be
published on October 31st.
His other works include CATHERINE CARMIER and
stories that have appeared in magazines and anthologies
including SOUTHERN WRITING IN THE
SIXTIES and THE BEST STORIES BY NEGRO
WRITERS.

You are invited · Admission is free

Baton Rouge was a dry town on Sundays, so I, along with some of the younger men would go across the Mississippi River to Port Allen, down to the White Eagle bar. The White Eagle was a rough place, and there were always fights, but I wanted to experience it all. One novel, *Of Love and Dust*, and a short story, "Three Men," came out of my experience at the White Eagle bar.

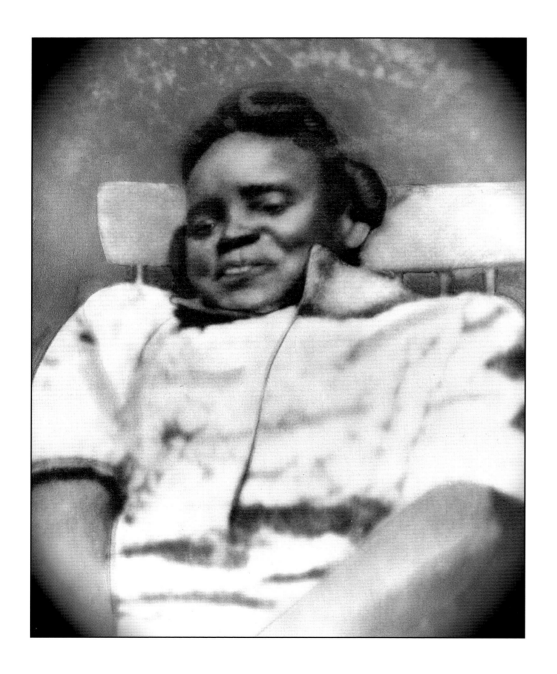

When people ask me who has been the greatest influence in my writing, I suppose they expect me to say another writer or a teacher. . . . But the greatest influence on me . . . has been my aunt, Miss Augusteen Jefferson. Not only for what she taught me with words . . . but she showed me, without the use of her legs, that I could do almost anything with those twenty-six letters if I would only work hard enough at it.

MISS JANE PITTMAN FOUNTAIN

donated by:

THE FREDDIE THOMAS FOUNDATION

During the time I was writing, I heard the voices . . . of my Louisiana people. I think that after I got really moving, Miss Jane's voice just followed through. I hate to say things like "I heard voices," because people would think I'm nuts. But certainly when I sat down at the desk, the voice took over again, and I started where I left off from the day before. It was almost the easiest book to write.

One character, Albert Cluveau, is based on a man who actually existed. In 1903, a Cajun assassin killed a black professor on the river. That was a story that the people told all my life . . . I visited the Parlange mansion, and met Madame Parlange, an old lady of about eighty-something, and she read the book [about Miss Jane Pittman]. She remembered these terrible Cajun assassinations and she told me that she knew exactly whom I'd based it on. This man, who would kill for whomever was paying him, was quite friendly toward people. He'd sit around and talk about his killings. Since I heard that he did these things, that's the way I put him in the book.

He was one of the people I had in mind when I was writing *The Autobiography of Miss Jane Pittman*, and especially when I was writing *A Gathering of Old Men*. In fact, he is the man whom I dedicated the book to posthumously—he would squat, not sit, on the porch by the door and drink and talk while I would lean back against a post, listening to him. He knew my grandparents' grandparents and all the others, white and black, who lived on that plantation the first eighty years of the twentieth century.

When I am writing a book, I never think about who the characters are going to be and how they will react to one another. If I have white characters, I try to make them as real as I possibly can, and if there are black characters I just try to make them as true as I possibly can. I never think about their liking or loving or disliking or loving or hating one another. We all have much more in common than we have differences. I would say that about people all over the world. They don't know how much in common they have.

I remember back in the sixties when all the violence was going on in the southern states . . . I would sit at my desk till I had written a perfect page. I would show the Bull Connors and the Faubuses, the Wallaces and the Thurmonds that I could do anything with those twenty-six letters given to them by their ancestors—not mine—but do more with those letters to help not only my race, but also my country, than they could ever do to destroy it.

Black students are always asking me, "Why do so many of your young men of vision die in your novels? You seem to kill off the braver ones. Are you trying to discourage us from trying?" I tell them that my young men die because they're not *supposed* to have vision. They're *supposed* to accept the status quo. . . . The young men in my novels and short stories who die cannot wait until others change the condition, because the condition then may not ever be changed.

An elementary school student once asked me if I would write all my life. I told her that on my deathbed that I would have a pen and a clipboard in my lap. She said nobody dies like that anymore.

I think of myself as a writer who happens to draw from his environment to express what his life is, what his heritage is. I try to put that down on paper.

Oprah Winfrey asked what I try to reach for in my writing. And I said something to this effect: I try to create characters with character to help develop my own character and maybe the character of the reader who might read me.

The 1993
John Dos Passos
Prize for Literature

will be presented to

ERNEST J. GAINES

Thursday, Sept. 15, 1994
8:00 p.m.
Wygal Auditorium
Longwood College

I don't need public attention, I'm not interested in written criticism of my work, but public attention is gratifying.

Fellowship of Southern Writers
Biennial Convocation, April 2, 1993
Chattanooga, Tennessee

Maybe sometime in the future I will write a good book, or publish a good book, about California. But I doubt that I will be able to do it until I have gotten rid of this Louisiana thing that drives me, yet I hope I never will get rid of that Louisiana thing. I hope I'm able to write about Louisiana for the rest of my life.

I think for the rest of my life I'll have something to write about Louisiana. I haven't touched the surface yet. I have so much to do.

LEGACY

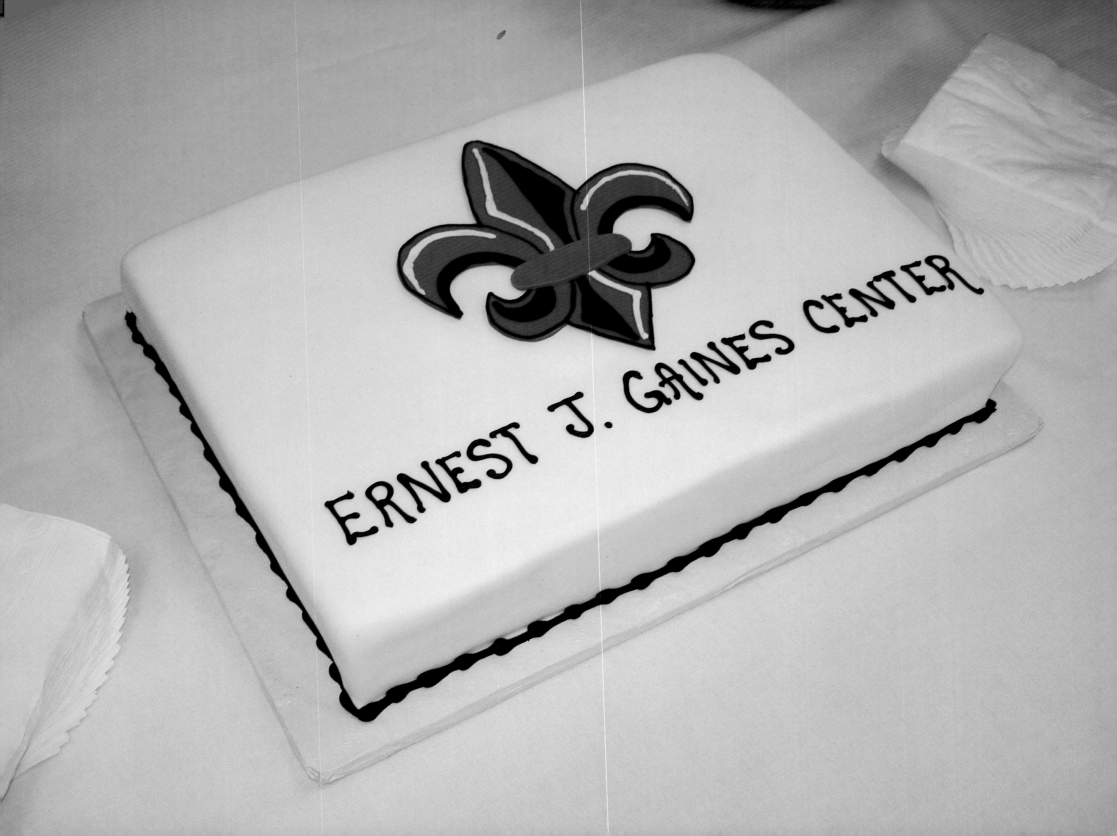

When I read Gaines, the poet said,
The sky is not gray, but gold.

~ Isaac Black

On Super Bowl Sunday 1981, Ernest J. Gaines received a telegram from University of Southwestern Louisiana (now University of Louisiana at Lafayette) offering him a position at this university. When he decided to return to Louisiana as our Visiting Writer-in-Residence, the sky was certainly gold over our university community.

For the last twenty-seven years, we have been privileged to be major benefactors of Ernest Gaines's time, energy, and generosity. He has contributed immeasurably to Creative Writing at The University of Louisiana at Lafayette while continuing to build an international reputation on the merits of his artistic accomplishments.

Gaines's reputation as a writer and artist is secure. Equally secure is his reputation as a man, as a teacher, as a colleague, as a friend, as a person passionately devoted to his people and his home state. He has deep concern for the land and the people who provided him with the roots of his artistic vision.

This concern is apparent in his quiet activism in preserving and refurbishing the cemetery on Riverlake Plantation where his ancestors, friends, and a brother are buried. He and his wife, Dianne, serve as President and Secretary of the Mount Zion River Lake Cemetery Association in Cherie Quarters, Oscar, Louisiana. The Gaines ask friends, family, and students to join them for a graveyard homecoming, or beautification day, at the cemetery on the last Saturday of October each year, the week-end before All Saints Day. In a traditional gathering, people come together to pull weeds, plant flowers, whitewash the tombs, eat, drink, and talk among the graves—remembering the past and rejoicing in its connection with the community of the present. The cemetery is a peaceful sanctuary, surrounded by sugarcane fields. This is also the time of "grinding," the sugarcane harvest in southern Louisiana. Ernest Gaines may peel a few stalks of sugarcane and instruct a young child or a new graduate student the proper way to chew it and spit out the pulp, something he remembers from his own childhood growing up in the plantation quarters.

Ernest Gaines has said that his great obsession was to get the property where his ancestors are buried and to maintain the cemetery, where he wants to be buried among the unmarked graves of his people. His writing has given him the power to determine how his people will be remembered. Gaines's narratives of his people have become stories of identity, stories of one's people. Gaines recognized the injustices to his people, and he addressed those injustices in his writing with a gentle but powerful anger. Perhaps more importantly, he recognized the worth of his people. He saw in them something worth writing about, something worth remembering—their character, their concern for others, their ability to survive with dignity, their belief in him and what his future could be. Gaines's stories give us a cultural narrative of the people he knew so well, a history of their lives and who they really were.

Ernest J. Gaines's legacy as a writer began with the legacy he received from his people. Along with his culture's legacy of poverty and injustice, he also received a strong legacy of personal dignity. Using the language of his community, he has made this place and these people a model for the simple but universal rights to one's own humanity, one's own dignity, one's own voice. By giving voice to those who traditionally had no voice outside of the ex-slave quarters, Gaines continues to fulfill his intent from the beginning of his writing career: to give voice to an unvoiced people, giving them the power to affirm their own existence.

Marcia Gaudet

When I started teaching at [UL in 1981], I was near this place, and I was always coming back, always coming back here and talking to the old people, and when my wife and I had the opportunity to buy a part of this plantation, of course we jumped at the chance and built a house here. I feel that I am still close to the people, my ancestors. They're buried about three-quarters of mile in the cemetery back here.

My brothers' children, and my brothers' and sister's grandchildren will be able to come here and say, "Our people were slaves here at one time." I wanted to preserve this place for the people buried back there, because without those people buried back there, I would not be a writer.

New Orleans, New Orleans,
New Orleans,
you will come back.
But will you be my
New Orleans . . .
I doubt it.

Katrina and the
politicians
have made you a
different New Orleans
forever.

THE MOUNT ZION RIVER LAKE CEMETERY ASSOCIATION,INC.
P.O.BOX 81
OSCAR,LOUISIANA 70762

OCTOBER 12,2005

Dear Friends and Relatives:

It is that time of year again as we approach Les Tous Saintes (All Saints Day) in this beautiful fall weather that we begin to prepare for our annual Beautification Day at the Cemetery in Cherie Quarters. It is a time of fellowship and camaraderie that we all look forward to. We hope that you will be able to join us on Saturday, October 29,2005 from 8:00 AM to 2:00 PM.

Hurricane Katrina did some damage to the trees,but Rita did more. We have started cleaning up, but will need strong men with chain saws to help get the bigger limbs out of the way. As in years past, we will provide some whitewash and plants. We ask that you bring whatever you can to help in the cleanup; rakes, shovels, buckets, rags and paint rollers or brushes.

At the end of the day, we will celebrate with a delicious meal prepared by Barbara Overstreet. We sincerely hope that you will join us.

Best Regards,

Ernest J.Gaines, President

In terms of how I want my epitaph to read, I want it to express what I want to do for the rest of eternity:

"To lie with those who have no mark."

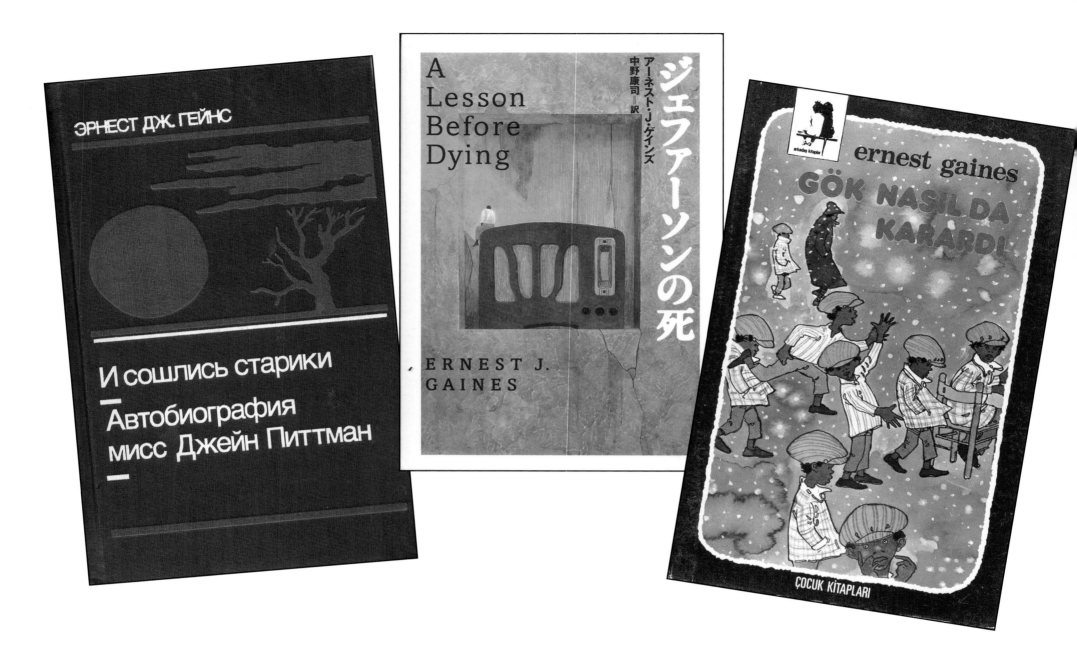

It's good to fail and not reach that high point that you are aiming at. It is best to die not ever having reached that peak because you are dead if you do reach it. I know I've never reached it. I suspect I will die trying.

"I think that Mr. Gaines is one of the greatest authors of our time. I always wanted to go to Louisiana and see the world of the works of Mr. Gaines. At last, my dream came true."

~ Professor Hitoshi Namekata, Metropolitan College, Tokyo, Japan
to Reese Fuller, *Lafayette Advertiser*.

My church is the oak tree. My church is the river. My church is walking right down the cane field road, on the headland between rows of sugarcane. That's my church. I can talk to God there as well as I can talk to him in Notre Dame. I think he's in one of those cane rows as much as he is in Notre Dame.

My six words of advice to writers are: 'Read, read, read, write, write, write.' Writing is a lonely job; you have to read, and then you must sit down at the desk and write. There is no one there to tell you when to write, what to write, or how to write.

Someone met me the other day . . . and said, "I'm so exasperated with *Catherine Carmier*! Why'd you leave us hanging there at the end, the way you did? . . . You're going to have to write a sequel!"

I said, "The sequel is that Dianne and I got married!"

Several feet away from where I sat under the tree was a hill of bull grass. I doubted that I had looked at it once in all the time that I had been sitting there. I probably would not have noticed it at all had a butterfly, a yellow butterfly with dark specks like ink dots on its wings, not lit there. What had brought it there? There was no odor that I could detect to have attracted it. There were other places where it could have rested—there was the wire fence on either side of the road, there were weeds along both ditches with strong fragrances, there were flowers just a short distance away in Pichot's yard—so why did it light on a hill of bull grass that offered it nothing? I watched closely, the way it opened its wings and closed them, the way it opened its wings again, fluttered, closed its wings for a second or two, then opened them again and flew away. I watched it fly over the ditch and down into the quarter, I watched it until I could not see it anymore.

~ Grant Wiggins, *A Lesson Before Dying*.

LAGNIAPPE

(something thrown in, gratis, for good measure.)

Quotation Sources

Page x. Interview with Marcia Gaudet and Darrell Bourque, *Mozart and Leadbelly* (eds. Marcia Gaudet and Reggie Young, Knopf, 2005), 140.

Page 19. Interview with Patricia Rickels, *Conversations with Ernest Gaines* (ed. John Lowe, UP of Mississippi, 1995), 132.

Page 23. "Writing A Lesson Before Dying," *Mozart and Leadbelly*, 54.

Page 24. Interview with Margaret R. Knight, *Conversations with Ernest Gaines*, 69.

Page 27. Lyrics from traditional spiritual "I Shall Not be Moved." Epigraph for "Just Like a Tree," *Bloodline* (Dial Press, 1968), 221.

Page 28. Unpublished interview with Jane Bonin, 1980s.

Page 29. Johnny Paul, *A Gathering of Old Men* (Knopf, 1983), 92.

Page 30. Interview with Charles H. Rowell "This Louisiana Thing That Drives Me," *Callaloo* 1:3 (1978), 40.

Page 33. Interview with Forrest Ingram and Barbara Steinberg, *Conversations with Ernest Gaines*, 39.

Page 34. *Porch Talk with Ernest Gaines*, Marcia Gaudet and Carl Wooton (LSU Press, 1990), 21.

Page 36. "Meeting Ernest Gaines," Interview with NEH Chair Bill Ferris, http://www.neh.gov/news/humanities/1998-07/gaines.html

Page 37. "A Very Big Order: Reconstructing Identity," *Mozart and Leadbelly*, 32-33.

Page 38. Miss Jane, *The Autobiography of Miss Jane Pittman* (Dial Press, 1971), 145.

Page 39. "The Last Regionalist?", Interview with Rose Anne Brister, *Callaloo* 26:3, (2003), 551.

Page 40. Interview with Charles H. Rowell, *Callaloo* (1978), 40.

Page 41. *Porch Talk with Ernest Gaines*, 37.

Page 43. Unpublished interview with Wiley Cash, 2006.

Page 46. "Mozart and Leadbelly," *Mozart and Leadbelly*, 24-25.

Page 47. Revised from "Miss Jane and I," *Mozart and Leadbelly*, 12.

Page 48. "Aunty and the Black Experience in Louisiana," *Mozart and Leadbelly*, 46.

Page 49. "Writing A Lesson Before Dying," *Mozart and Leadbelly*, 62.

Page 51. "Mozart and Leadbelly," *Mozart and Leadbelly*, 26-27.

Page 52. "Aunty and the Black Experience in Louisiana," *Mozart and Leadbelly*, 45.

Page 54. "Meeting Ernest Gaines," Interview with NEH Chair Bill Ferris, http://www.neh.gov/news/humanities/1998-07/gaines.html

Page 55. "Meeting Ernest Gaines," Interview with NEH Chair Bill Ferris, http://www.neh.gov/news/humanities/1998-07/gaines.html

Page 56. Revised from "Miss Jane and I," *Mozart and Leadbelly*, 21.

Page 57. "Meeting Ernest Gaines," Interview with NEH Chair Bill Ferris, http://www.neh.gov/news/humanities/1998-07/gaines.html

Page 58. "Aunty and the Black Experience in Louisiana," *Mozart and Leadbelly*, 48.

Page 59. "Aunty and the Black Experience in Louisiana," *Mozart and Leadbelly*, 49-50.

Page 60. "Introduction," *This Louisiana Thing That Drives Me*, xvii.

Page 61. Revised from *Porch Talk with Ernest Gaines*, 81.

Page 62. "Writing A Lesson Before Dying," *Mozart and Leadbelly*, 62.

Page 63. Unpublished interview with Jane Bonin, 1980s.

Page 65. Interview with Charles H. Rowell, *Callaloo* (1978), 40.

Page 67. Interview with Dan Tooker and Roger Hofheins. *Conversations with Ernest Gaines*, 111.

Page 69. "When I Read Ernest Gaines," by Isaac Black. *Callaloo* 1978.

Page 71. "The Scribe of River Lake Plantation," Interview by Anne Gray Brown, *Southern Quarterly* 44:1 (2006), 17.

Page 72. Unpublished interview with Wiley Cash, 2006.

Page 73. "Where Have You Gone New Orleans?" *National Geographic* 210:2 (August 2006), 57.

Page 75. Unpublished interview with Marcia Gaudet and Reggie Scott Young, 2007.

Page 76. "Reflections of a Serious Writer," Interview with Cindy Urrea, *Acadiana Profile* (November 1997).

Page 77. Professor Hitoshi Namekata quoted by R. Reese Fuller, "An Ernest Scholar," *The Lafayette Advertiser*, August 25, 2003. http://www.reesefuller.com/words/20030825.html

Page 78. "Talking with Ernest J. Gaines," interview with Marcia Gaudet, *Louisiana Literature* 16.1 (Spring 1999), 65.

Page 81. "An Interview with Ernest J. Gaines," Jennifer Levasseur and Kevin Rabalais, *The Missouri Review* (1999), 97.

Page 82. Revised from an interview with John Lowe. *Conversations with Ernest Gaines*, 302.

Page 84. Grant, *A Lesson Before Dying*, Knopf (1993), 251-252.

Photograph Credits

Front Cover: Ernest J. Gaines in Cherie Quarters, River Lake Plantation, 1986. Photo by Marcia Gaudet.

Page viii. Louisiana Center for the Book Ernest J Gaines Louisiana Writer Award Broadside, 2000. Reproduced with permission of the State Library of Louisiana.

Page ix. Wendell Berry and Gaines, 2007. Photo by Wiley Cash.

Page x. Scenes from River Lake Plantation, 1960s. Photos by Ernest J. Gaines.

Page xi. Gaines in high school. Photo courtesy of Ernest J Gaines.

Page xii. Gaines in Cherie Quarters, 1986. Photo by Marcia Gaudet.

Page xiii. Gaines and David Biben, 1960s. Photo courtesy of Ernest J. Gaines.

Page xiv. Gaines at book signing. Photo courtesy of Ernest J. Gaines.

Page xv. Gaines in Baton Rouge, 1960s. Photo courtesy of Ernest J. Gaines.

Page xvi. Gaines in 1990s. Photo courtesy of Ernest J. Gaines.

Page xvii. Gaines at False River, 1991. Photo by Dianne Gaines.

Page 19. Girls and women on Alma Plantation, 1934. Courtesy of Library of Congress, Prints & Photographs Division, Lomax Collection, Photo by Alan Lomax.

Page 20. Oak tree on Hwy 1 in Lakeland, near Oscar, known as "Miss Jane's Oak," 1960s. It was the inspiration for the oak tree in *The Autobiography of Miss Jane Pittman*. Photo by Ernest J. Gaines.

Page 22. Plantation workers' houses in Cherie Quarters, 1960s. Photo by Ernest J. Gaines.

Page 23. Mt. Zion Baptist Church in Cherie Quarters, 1986. Photo by Marcia Gaudet.

Page 24. Gaines in San Francisco, 1960s. Photo courtesy of Ernest J. Gaines.

Page 25. River Lake Plantation House, Oscar, Louisiana, 1960s. Photo by Ernest J. Gaines.

Page 26. Trees in Cherie Quarters, 2006. Photo by Wiley Cash.

Page 27. Woman on Alma Plantation, False River, Louisiana, 1934. Courtesy of Library of Congress, Prints & Photographs Division, Lomax Collection, Photo by Alan Lomax.

Page 28. Children on Allen Plantation, 1940. Courtesy of the Library of Congress, Prints & Photographs Division, Farm Security Administration Collection. Photo by Marion Post Wolcott.

Page 29. Tractor/harvester on River Lake Plantation, 2006. Photo by Wiley Cash. Gaines in Mt. Zion Cemetery, 1991. Photo by Dianne Gaines.

Page 30. Baptist congregation, Louisiana, 1934. Courtesy of Library of Congress, Prints & Photographs Division, Lomax Collection, Photo by Alan Lomax.

Page 31. African American workers on porch, Alma Plantation, 1934. Courtesy of Library of Congress, Prints & Photographs Division, Lomax Collection, Photo by Alan Lomax.

Page 32. False River with the Gaines's pier, 2007. Photo by Reggie Scott Young.

Page 33. Gaines walking beside a lake in Baton Rouge, near women fishing. 1960s. Photo courtesy of Ernest J. Gaines.

Page 34. Gaines in front of Mt. Zion Baptist Church, Cherie Quarters, 1987. Photo by Carl Wooton.

Page 35. Interior of renovated Mt. Zion Church, 2006. Photo by Wiley Cash.

Page 36. Group of men with Gaines, on porch in Cherie Quarters, River Lake Plantation, 1960s. Photo by Joe Williams, courtesy of Ernest J. Gaines.

Page 37. Young boy in Cherie Quarters, 1960s. Photo by Ernest J. Gaines.

Page 38. Miss Jane's oak tree, 2007. Photo by Wiley Cash.

Page 39. Gaines in San Francisco, 1970s. Photo courtesy of Ernest J. Gaines.

Page 40. Some of Gaines's nieces and nephews, children of his brother Eugene, in front of their house in New Roads, late 1960s or early 1970s. Photo by Ernest J. Gaines.

Page 41. Gaines peeling sugarcane, Cemetery Beautification Day, 2004. Photo by Marcia Gaudet. Sugarcane fields on River Lake Plantation, 2006. Photo by Wiley Cash.

Page 43. Gaines reading from Bloodline, late 1960s. Photo courtesy of Ernest J. Gaines.

Page 44. Covers of books by Gaines. Photo by James D. Wilson, Jr.

Page 46. James Meredith escorted to class by U.S. marshals, Oxford, Mississippi, 1962. Courtesy of Library of Congress, Prints & Photographs Division, New York World-Telegram &

Sun Collection, photo by Marion S. Trikosko [reproduction number LC-U9-8556-24 (9-8)].

Page 47. Letter for receiving Honorable Mention in the Air Force Short Story Contest and award check for the Short Story Contest on Guam. Photos by Reggie Scott Young.

Page 48. Dorothea Oppenheimer, Gaines's literary agent. Photo courtesy of Ernest J Gaines. Manuscript page from "The Turtles" and cover of *Catherine Carmier*. Photos by Reggie Scott Young.

Page 49. Gaines in his apartment in San Francisco, with books in the background, late 1970s. Self photo by Ernest J Gaines.

Page 50. Poster for a reading by Gaines in San Francisco, 1967. Photo by Reggie Scott Young.

Page 51. White Eagle Bar, 1960s. Photo by Ernest J Gaines.

Page 52. Miss Augusteen Jefferson, early 1950s. Photo by Julia McVay (grandmother of Ernest Gaines).

Page 53. Dedication of the Miss Jane Pittman Drinking Fountain, Rochester, New York, 1989. Photo courtesy of Ernest J. Gaines.

Page 54. Cicely Tyson as Miss Jane Pittman in the 1974 CBS movie *The Autobiography of Miss Jane Pittman*. Photos courtesy of Ernest J. Gaines.

Page 55. Illustration of murder of black professor from Japanese edition of *The Autobiography of Miss Jane Pittman*. Scan by Reggie Scott Young. Photo of grave stone of Petrus E. L. Plantevigne, on the site of Zion Travelers Baptist Church, Highway 1, along False River. Professor Plantevigne opened a school for African Americans near this site in 1900. The school closed after his assassination in 1903. Photo by Marcia Gaudet, 1986.

Page 56. Mr. Walter ("Pete") Zeno, at River Lake Plantation Cherie Quarters, 1968. Photos by Ernest J. Gaines.

Page 57. Walter Breaux, Ernest J. Gaines, and Richard Whaley, on the set of the 1987 CBS movie A Gathering of Old Men, at Laurel Valley Plantation, Thibodaux, Louisiana. Photo courtesy of Ernest J. Gaines.

Page 58. Gaines sitting on floor of his home library in San Francisco, late 1970s. Photo by Jim Santana, courtesy of Ernest J. Gaines.

Page 59. Gaines, late 1960s. Photo courtesy of Ernest J. Gaines.

Page 60. Gaines at a reading and booksigning, 1970s. Photo courtesy of Ernest J. Gaines. Gaines with James Bond III on the set of the television movie *The Sky Is Gray*, 1980. Photo courtesy of Ernest J. Gaines.

Page 61. Gaines in maroon shirt, with notebook. Photo courtesy of Ernest J. Gaines.

Page 62. Gaines with Oprah Winfrey at River Lake Plantation, 1997. Ernest and Dianne Gaines with President Bill Clinton and First Lady Hillary Clinton, Washington, D.C., 2000. Photos courtesy of Ernest J. Gaines.

Page 63. Gaines with Ralph Ellison, on the occasion of Ellison's receiving the title Chevalier de l'Ordre des Arts et des Lettres, 1970. Fellowship of Southern Writers, 1993. John Dos Passos Award, photo by Reggie Scott Young.

Page 64. Gaines at his UL Lafayette Retirement Gala, January 15, 2005. Photo by Blaine Faul. Poster of Gaines's Deep South reading, April 2005. Photos by Reggie Scott Young.

Page 65. Gaines on railroad tracks in Pointe Coupée Parish, 1960s. Photo courtesy of Ernest J. Gaines. Manuscript page of "My Uncle and the Fat Lady," 2007.

Page 67. Church pew in restored Mt. Zion Baptist Church, 2006. Photo by Wiley Cash.

Page 68. Cake at media event announcing the establishment of the Ernest J. Gaines Center, Dupre Library, UL Lafayette, March 2008. Photo by Wiley Cash.

Page 70. Home of Ernest and Dianne Gaines, Oscar, Louisiana, 2007. Photo by Reggie Scott Young.

Page 71. Mt. Zion Cemetery Beautification Day, 2003. Photo by Marcia Gaudet.

Page 72. Mt. Zion Cemetery, 2006. Photo by Wiley Cash. Children playing on graves, Mt. Zion Cemetery Beautification Day, 2003. Photo by Marcia Gaudet.

Page 73. New Orleans after Hurricane Katrina, September 2005. Photos by Donald Begneaud.

Page 74. Cemetery Beautification Day letter from Ernest J. Gaines, October 2005. Mt. Zion Cemetery Beautification Day, 2005. Photos by Reggie Scott Young.

Page 75. Graves in Mt. Zion Cemetery, 2009. Photo by Joseph Sanford.

Page 76. Book covers of three translations of Gaines's works, left to right: *A Gathering of Old Men* (Russian), *A Lesson Before Dying* (Japanese), *The Sky Is Gray* (Turkish). Photos by Reggie Scott Young.

Page 77. Japanese professor and scholar Hitoshi Namekata, interviewing Ernest Gaines. Photos by Reggie Scott Young.

Page 78. "Negro family praying at graves of their relatives on All Saints' Day, New Roads, Louisiana," 1938. Courtesy of Library of Congress, Prints & Photographs Division, Farm Security Administration-Office of War Information Collection. Photo by Russell Lee. Gaines at Beautification Day, 2004. Photo by Reggie Scott Young. Sugarcane field, River Lake Plantation, 1960s. Photo by Ernest J. Gaines.

Page 79. Gaines on steps of Mt. Zion Baptist Church, 2008. Photo by Thomas Neff, Baton Rouge.

Page 80. Gaines rocking on his front porch, Oscar, Louisiana, 2007. Photo by David Humphreys, Baton Rouge.

Page 81. Gaines signing a book. Photo by Wiley Cash.

Page 82. Gaines at the site that will become the Ernest J. Gaines Center, Dupre Library, UL Lafayette, March 2008. Photo by Wiley Cash.

Page 83. Dianne Saulney Gaines at False River, 1991. Photo by Ernest J. Gaines.

Page 84. Gaines on steps to his apartment, San Francisco, 1963. Photo by Sam Bibbens.

Page 85. Yellow butterfly in Mt. Zion Cemetery, 1991. Photo by Ernest J. Gaines.

Page 86. Ernest Gaines and Reese Spooner in Cherie Quarters, 1982. Photo by Philip Gould.

Page 87. Photos courtesy of Ernest J. Gaines.

Page 88. Photos courtesy of Ernest J. Gaines.

Page 89. Gaines at UL Lafayette, 1980s. Photo by Doug Dugas. Gaines at his home in Lafayette, 1980s. Photo courtesy of Ernest J. Gaines.

Page 90. Gaines in Lafayette. Photo courtesy of Ernest J. Gaines.

Page 91. View from inside the church of Ernest Gaines walking from his house toward the church, 2005. Photo by Wiley Cash.

Page 95. Authors photo, May 2007. Clockwise from bottom left: Ernest J. Gaines, Wiley Cash, Reggie Scott Young, Marcia Gaudet. Photo by Charles W. Triche, III.

Rear Cover: Ernest J. Gaines in Mt. Zion Baptist Church, 2008. Photo by Joseph Sanford, Pelican Pictures.

ERNEST J. GAINES CENTER

The Ernest J. Gaines Center at University of Louisiana at Lafayette, established in 2008, is an international center for scholarship on Ernest Gaines and his work. The center honors the work of UL Lafayette's Writer-in-Residence *Emeritus* and provides a space for scholars and students to work with the Gaines papers and manuscripts. Gaines's generous donation of his early papers and manuscripts (through 1983) and some artifacts to Edith Garland Dupré Library provided the foundation for the center's collection. The center also anticipates acquiring the remainder of Gaines's papers.

Along with the Gaines papers and published scholarship, the Ernest J. Gaines Center can also anticipate the donation of extensive research papers, manuscripts and tape-recorded interviews of Gaines scholars. The center will expand the collection on Ernest Gaines to include all books, journal articles, essays, interviews, theses and dissertations on Ernest Gaines and his work. In addition, it will include a complete collection of all the published translations of Ernest Gaines's writings. It will be the site of the only complete collection of Ernest Gaines scholarship in the world.

The Ernest J. Gaines Center will also coordinate other activities related to research and scholarship on the work of Ernest J. Gaines, and it may be extended to research on other Louisiana African American writers. The first of these activities will be an Ernest J. Gaines Scholars Conference at UL Lafayette, bringing in major scholars for presentations and inviting other scholars to do presentations and discussions in sessions, all focused on Ernest Gaines's fiction.

Another activity of the center will be the Ernest J. Gaines Speakers and Writers Series. This series will continue to bring major scholars and writers to UL Lafayette and will focus on the work of creative writers and eminent scholars.

While UL Lafayette has contributed $500,000 to establish the center, the activities of the center will also depend on philanthropic contributions. To begin this fundraising campaign, all royalties from *This Louisiana Thing That Drives Me: The Legacy of Ernest J. Gaines* will go to The Ernest J. Gaines Center. In addition, a deluxe numbered edition of the book, signed by Ernest J. Gaines and the other authors, will be given to the first 100 contributors of $5,000 or more to the center.